Iona Journal

wild goose publications  www.ionabooks.com

Paperback edition first published 2011
Wild Goose Publications
Suite 9, Fairfield, 1048 Govan Road
Glasgow G51 4XS, Scotland
A division of Iona Community Trading CIC
Limited Company Reg. No. SC156678

www.ionabooks.com

ISBN 978-1-84952-202-1

Copyright © Wild Goose Publications
Photograph © David Coleman

All rights reserved. No part of this publication may be reproduced
in any form or by any means including photocopying or any information storage
or retrieval system, without written permission from the publisher via PLSclear.com.

Overseas distribution:
Australia: Willow Connection Pty Ltd, 1/13 Kell Mather Drive, Lennox Head NSW 2478
New Zealand: Pleroma, Higginson Street, Otane 4170, Central Hawkes Bay

Printed by Bell & Bain, Thornliebank, Glasgow

God's spirit permeates 'every blessed thing'

George MacLeod

> Follow the light you have
> and pray for more light
>
> George MacLeod

> People come to Iona looking for peace and quiet,
> and go away seeking peace and justice
>
> A volunteer with the Iona Community

To work is to pray

Benedictine saying

Be still, and know that I am God

Psalm 46:10

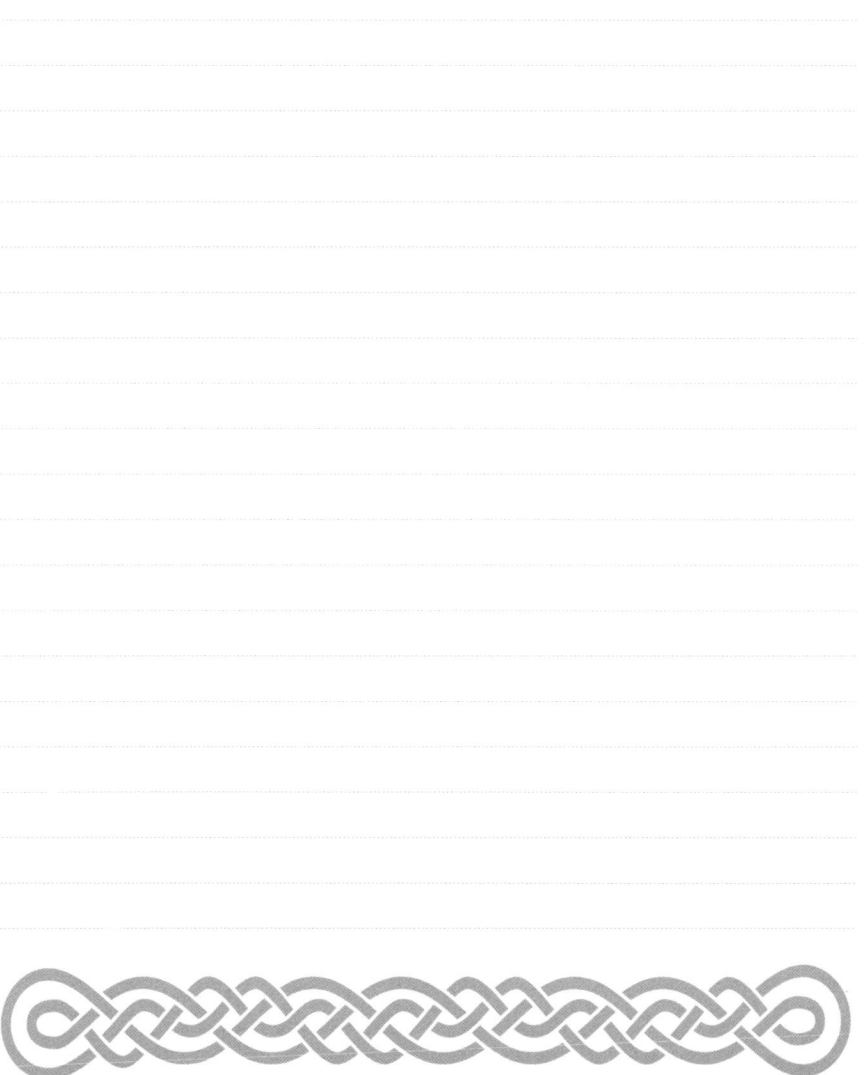

Iona is a thin place – just a piece of tissue paper between things spiritual and material

George MacLeod

> Jesus wasn't crucified on an altar
> between two silver candlesticks
> but on a garbage heap between two thieves
>
> George MacLeod

**Eat and drink together,
talk and laugh together,
enjoy life together.**

**but never call it friendship
until you have wept together**

An African saying

The power of love is greater than the love of power

George MacLeod

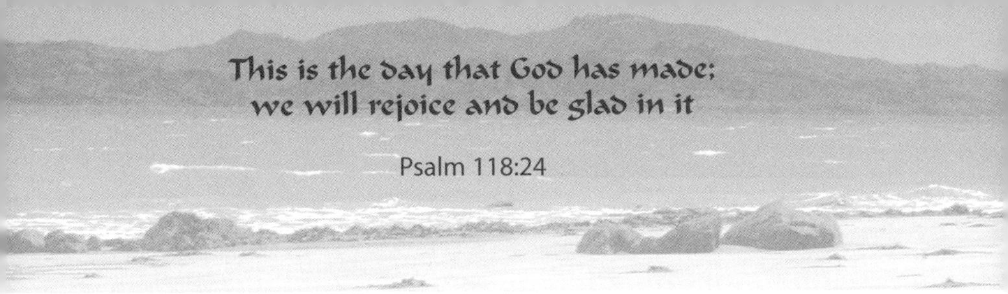

This is the day that God has made; we will rejoice and be glad in it

Psalm 118:24

Love and peace come together; justice and peace join hands

Psalm 85:10

> In Iona of my heart, Iona of my love,
> Instead of monks' voices shall be lowing of cattle,
> But ere the world come to an end
> Iona shall be as it was
>
> Attributed to St Columba

May God be a bright flame before me,
be a guiding star above me,
be a smooth path below me,

> **be thou a kindly shepherd behind me,
> today, tonight and forever**
>
> Attributed to St Columba

Light a candle, don't just curse the darkness

Chinese saying

Deep peace of the running wave to you.
Deep peace of the flowing air to you.
Deep peace of the quiet earth to you.

> Deep peace of the shining stars to you,
> Deep peace of the Son of peace to you
>
> Celtic blessing

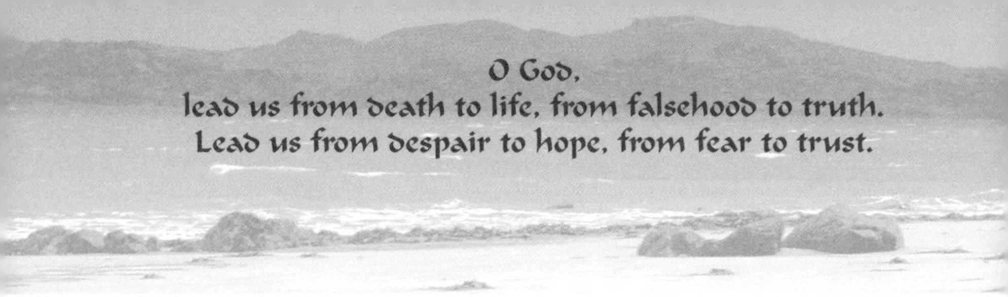

O God,
lead us from death to life, from falsehood to truth.
Lead us from despair to hope, from fear to trust.

> Lead us from hate to love, from war to peace.
> Let peace fill our hearts, our world, our universe.
>
> — Universal prayer for peace

> Take us outside, O Christ, outside holiness,
> out to where soldiers curse and nations clash
> at the crossroads of the world
>
> George MacLeod

A blessing on you who hunger for justice, you shall be satisfied

Matthew 5:6

> And what does the Lord require of you but to do justice,

*and to love kindness,
and to walk humbly with your God?*

Micah 6:8

Peace between nations,
peace between neighbours.

peace between lovers,
in love of the God of life

From a Celtic prayer

Each thing we have received,
From you it came;
Each thing for which we hope,

> From your love it will come;
> Each thing we enjoy,
> It is of your bounty
>
> Gaelic prayer

> Lord, make us instruments of your peace.
> Where there is hatred, let us sow love,
> Where there is injury, pardon,

> Where there is doubt, faith,
> Where there is despair, hope,
> Where there is sadness, joy.
>
> St Francis

O Christ, there is no plant in the ground
But it is full of your virtue.
There is no form in the strand
But it is full of your blessing.
There is no life in the sea,
There is no creature in the ocean,

There is nothing in the heavens
But proclaims your goodness.
There is no bird on the wing,
There is no star in the sky,
There is nothing beneath the sun
But proclaims your goodness.

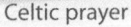
Celtic prayer

Invisible we see You, Christ beneath us.
With earthly eyes we see beneath us stones and dust
and dross, fit subjects for the analyst's table.
But with the eye of faith, we know You uphold.
In You all things consist and hang together:

> The very atom is light energy,
> The grass is vibrant,
> The rocks pulsate.
> All is in flux; turn but a stone and an angel moves.
>
> George MacLeod

> You are an island in the sea, O God,
> you are a hill on the shore,
> you are a star in the darkness,
> you are a staff to the weak

From the *Carmina Gaedelica*

> Lord, to those who hunger, give bread.
> And to those who have bread, give the hunger for justice.
>
> Latin American prayer

> Personally consumed of the here and now,
> we must discover God as here and now
>
> George MacLeod

> I have come in order that you might have life –
> life in all its fullness
>
> John 10:10

If the only prayer you ever said was 'Thank you' – you would have said all the prayers

Meister Eckhart

For work and worship
prayer and action
being and doing

for sharing stories and for sharing beauty beyond words
for long walks alone and for pilgrimages together

for the sound of the ferry and for the echo of church bells
for quiet time and for the wild dance of the spirit
for storms that pass and for rainbows
for daffodils in bloom and for a night full of stars ...
Thank you, God

From *Blessed Be Our Table*

May God write a message upon your heart
bless and direct you,
then send you out
living letters of the Word

from *Iona Abbey Worship Book*

Often goes Christ in the stranger's guise

From the Celtic rune of hospitality

The Iona Community is:

An international, ecumenical Christian movement working for justice and peace, the rebuilding of community and the renewal of worship.

Our Community was founded in Glasgow in 1938 by Rev George MacLeod. A visionary and a social reformer, MacLeod was driven by a belief that faith is grounded in action. In rebuilding the ruined accommodation at Iona Abbey, trainee ministers and unemployed workers lived, worked and worshipped together.

We are now about 280 Members and more than 2,000 Associate Members, Young Adults and Friends across the world. We remain true to that founding vision – sharing common work and community as we pursue justice and peace, in Scotland and beyond.

For information on the Iona Community contact:
Phone: 0141 429 7281
e-mail: admin@iona.org.uk; web: www.iona.org.uk

For information on Wild Goose Publications contact:
Phone: 0141 429 7281
e-mail: admin@ionabooks.com; web: www.ionabooks.com

For enquiries about visiting Iona, please contact:
Phone: 01681 700404
e-mail: admin@iona.org.uk

For enquiries about visiting Camas, please contact:
Phone: 01681 700367
e-mail: camasprogramme@iona.org.uk